A Bit Of History
JESUS Weeps

But GOD forbid that I should glory, save in the Cross of our LORD JESUS CHRIST, by WHOM the world is crucified unto me, and I unto the world.
(Galatians 6:14 KJV)

For HE hath made HIM to be sin, for us, WHO knew no sin; that we might be made the righteousness of GOD in HIM.
(2 Corinthians 5:21 KJV)

Bob Robinson

 www.trafford.com

North America & international
toll-free: 1 888 232 4444 (USA & Canada)
phone: 250 383 6864 ♦ fax: 250 383 6804 ♦ email: info@trafford.com

Foreword

Purpose of this book: The maximum number of people, worldwide, will receive a good report on Judgment Day.

I find that religion has a scientific approach that has been overlooked. Matthew 16:19 and 18:18 state: ***What you bind on Earth is bound in Heaven and what you loose on Earth is loosed in Heaven.*** Both Matthew 16:19 and 18:18 mean the same even though different words are used.

The Koran states the same: ***When you do good you do it to yourself and when you do evil you do it to yourself. Thus shall you be brought back to your LORD.***

Heaven co-exists with the world now on Earth.

Hell co-exists with the world now on Earth.

Yes, I realize that what I am claiming, in this book, does not fit the normal person's thinking. As far as I know I am the only one who believes as I do. However, there have been too many unusual events that I can no longer resist in having them published.

The first section of the book contains a brief history of the early Christian Church and many quotes from the Bible supporting my thinking.

The second section contains the events which occurred in my life, you might call it my testimony. I was warned, spiritually, early in conversion: ***"Do not exaggerate; MY deeds do not need to be exaggerated."***

The last section includes my conclusions.

Abbreviations

Hermas   *The Apostolic Fathers (second edition.)* Translated by Lightfoot and Harmer and edited by Michael W. Holmes.

TLB   Scripture quotations marked (TLB) are taken from *The Living Bible* copyright 1971. Used by permission of Tyndale House Publishers, Inc., Wheaton, IL 60189 All rights reserved.

RSV   *Revised Standard Version*

KJV   *King James Version*

NLT   Scripture quotations marked (NLT) are taken from *The Holy Bible, New Living translation,* copyright 1996. Used by permission of Tyndale House Publishers, Inc., Wheaton, IL 60189. All rights reserved.

NKJV   *New King James Version*

NAS   Naval Air Station

About the author

Bob was born near Thornburg, Iowa 27 September 1924; he graduated from Thornburg High School in 1942, a class of eight students. He enlisted in the Navy V-5 Fight Cadet program and completed two semesters at the University of Iowa before being called to active duty in the Navy, August or September of 1943

He graduated, as an Ensign at NAS Pensacola, FL just as the war ended in September 1945. He remained in the Navy, serving aboard the aircraft carrier *USS Franklin D. Roosevelt* as a Helldiver pilot, was discharged from active duty in December 1946.

Bob was engaged to be married to Dottie in February 1946. He received a letter from Dottie as he returned to NAS Norfolk, aboard the carrier, from the Mediterranean Sea. She wanted to return the ring.

Bob was active in the Navy Reserve until 1973. He retired as a Commander after serving two tours as Commanding Office of two Reserve Patrol Squadrons.

From 1947 to 1973 Bob worked for his father, who was a Ford Dealer in What Cheer, Iowa. He had brief stints as a flight instructor and attempted a futile career in Life Insurance.

Bob married Patricia Davis in January 1947 and has three daughters; Lynn, Sandra and Karen.

Bob & Patricia moved to Fort Pierce, FL in 1973. He worked briefly for the fixed base operator in Stuart, FL and then opened his own flight school at the Stuart airport. He sold the business in 1985 and managed the school for two years. He quit flying in 1987 and went to Hobe Sound Bible College for two semesters.

Bob moved back to Iowa full time in 2001. He considers What Cheer his home, unless the LORD sends him back to the Stuart, FL area.

A Bit Of History
JESUS Weeps

FIRST SECTION
Matthew 18:18

Emperor Constantine, the first Christian Roman emperor, issued this edict:

All judges, city-people and craftsmen shall rest on the venerable day of the Sun. But countrymen may without hindrance attend to agriculture, since it often happens that this is the most suitable day for sowing grain or planting vines, so that the opportunity afforded by divine providence may not be lost, for the right season is short. (Erdmans' Handbook to the History of Christianity, page 144)

This occurred on 7 March 321 CE. The Christian CHURCH leaders, at Rome, took advantage of his proclamation to officially, within the Roman CHURCH, to change the Sabbath to Sunday. The early Christians resented the restrictions the Jews had placed on the Sabbath Day and welcomed a day that separated them from the Hebrews.

About the same time the Christian leaders, at Rome, also decided that they had the privilege of annulling marriages. They used Matthew 16:19 for the authority to make the changes; JESUS had spoken these words to Peter:

"And I will give you the keys of the Kingdom of Heaven; whatever doors you lock on Earth shall be locked in Heaven; and whatever doors you open of Earth shall be open in Heaven." (Matthew 16:19 TLB)

The CHURCH leaders, at that time, interpreted the verse to apply only to Saint Peter and his successors. They claimed that it gave Peter and his successors the privilege of changing our CREATOR'S instructions as to how we were to live; therefore they could annul marriages and change the Sabbath Day. Very bad decisions!

In Matthew 18:18 JESUS spoke words meaning the same, as Matthew 16:19, to all HIS disciples:

"And I tell you this—whatever you bind on Earth is bound in Heaven, and whatever you free on Earth will be freed in Heaven." (Matthew 18:18 TLB)

"He who doth that which is right, doth it to his own behoof, and whoso doth evil, doth it to his own hurt. Hereafter, to your LORD shall ye be brought back." (Koran Sura 45:14)

A simple interpretation today would be: If we want GOD to prevent an auto accident, we must obey the traffic rules the best we can.

I find that Matthew 18:18 & 16:19 are as binding as Newton's Law of Motion which states: *For every action there is an equal and opposite reaction.*

These two verses from Matthew are the keys to Heaven on Earth in this our lifetime.

Following are examples of the correct meaning of Matthew 16:19 & 18:18, from the Bible, Gospel of Thomas and *The Shepherd of Hermas.*

OLD TESTAMENT

ONE

Adam & Eve were originally in the Garden of Eden, which represented Heaven. They did not follow GOD'S instructions so they were banned from Heaven on Earth.

And to Adam, GOD said, "Because you listened to your wife and ate the fruit when I told you not to, I have placed a curse upon the soil. All your life you will struggle to extract a living from it." (Genesis 3:17 TLB)

From that day on Adam & Eve, and mankind, have struggled to survive.

TWO

Joseph was sold, by his brothers, as a slave; consequently the entire Jewish race became slaves a few generations later.

So when traders (Midianites) came by his brothers pulled Joseph out of the well and sold him, to them for twenty pieces of silver, and they took him along to Egypt. (Genesis 37:28 TLB)

So the Egyptians made slaves of them and put brutal task-masters over them to wear them down under heavy burdens while building the store-cities Pithom and Raamses. (Exodus 1:11 TLB)

This example demonstrates that our sin is passed to our descendents.

THREE

The Pharaoh threatened to kill Moses, which caused the first-born Egyptians to die as a result.

"Get out of here and don't let me ever see you again," *Pharaoh shouted at Moses. "The day you do, you shall die."* (Exodus 10:28 TLB)

And that night, at midnight, JEHOVAH killed all the first-

born sons in the land of Egypt, from Pharaoh's oldest son to the oldest son of the captive in the dungeon; also all the firstborn of the cattle. (Exodus 12:29 TLB)

The people of a nation suffer when their leaders sin. The people of a congregation suffer when their leader sins or another member of a congregation, or any organization, sins unless they renounce the offense and limit their social contact.

FOUR

When Abram was ninety-nine years old, GOD appeared to him and told him, "I am the ALMIGHTY; obey ME and live as you should. I will prepare a contract between us, guaranteeing to make you into a mighty nation. In fact you shall be the father of not only one nation, but a multitude of nations!" (Genesis 17:1-4 TLB)

Please note: "obey ME and live as you should."

"If you will listen to the voice of the LORD your GOD, and obey it, and do what is right, then I will not make you suffer the diseases I send on the Egyptians, for I am the LORD WHO heals you." (Exodus 15:26 TLB)

The Promised Land was conditional; the Jews were to live as GOD wanted then to live.

The LORD OF HOSTS, the GOD of Israel says, Away with your offerings and sacrifices! It wasn't offerings and sacrifices I wanted from your fathers when I led them out of Egypt. That was not the point of MY command. But what I told them was: Obey ME and I will be your GOD and you shall be MY people; only do as I say and all shall be well! (Jeremiah 7:21-23 TLB)

This passage, from Jeremiah, is typical of the warnings given by the prophets in the Old Testament.

Finally, JESUS demonstrated the exact will of our

CREATOR. The Jews turn HIM down, resulting in this proclamation.

But as they came closer to Jerusalem and HE saw the city ahead, HE began to cry. "Eternal Peace was within your reach and you turned it down," HE wept, "and now it is too late. Your enemies will pile up earth against your walls and encircle you and close in on you, and crush you to the ground, and your children within you; your enemies will not leave one stone upon another— for you have rejected the opportunity GOD offered you."

Then HE entered the Temple and began to drive out the merchants from their stalls, saying to them, "The Scriptures declare, 'MY Temple is a place of prayer; but you have turned it into a den of thieves.'" (Luke 19:41-46 TLB)

JESUS included the words, *"your children within you,"* extends the prophecy eternally. And so it has been since 70 AD, when the Roman Army tore down the Temple and threw the Jews out of Jerusalem. The Zealots had taken over the leadership of Jerusalem from the Pharisee and Sadducees resulting in armed resistance to Rome, for the three and one-half years prior to the destruction of the Temple.

The only remedy is to accept JESUS as LORD and live as HE taught. JESUS cancelled the Promised Land Contract and Temple worship with these words and actions.

FIVE

So the LORD told Abraham, "I have heard that the people of Sodom and Gomorrah are utterly evil, and that everything they do is wicked. I am going down to see whether these reports are true or not. Then I will know." (Genesis 18:20_21 TLB)

"What relatives do you have here in the city?" the men asked. "Get them out of this place—sons-law, sons, daughters, or anyone else. For we will destroy the city completely. The stench

of the place has reached to Heaven and GOD has sent us to destroy it." (Genesis 19:12-13 TLB)

"Flee for your lives" the angels told him, "And don't look back. Escape to the mountains. Don't stay down here on the plain or you will die." (Genesis 19:17 TLB)

But Lot's wife looked back as she was following along behind him, and became a pillar of salt. (Genesis 19:26 TLB)

Lot's wife wanted to go back to the sinful community. She did not trust the LORD. This story demonstrates that we have to separate ourselves from those around us who are sinning. Since we live in a sinful world, that means a minimum of social contact with known sinners.

SIX

Now as it happened, Israel (Jacob) loved Joseph more than any of his other children because Joseph was born to him in his old age. So one day Jacob gave him a special gift—a brightly colored coat. His brothers of course noticed their father's partiality, and consequently hated Joseph; they couldn't say a kind word to him. (Genesis 37:3 TLB)

In this example GOD is demonstrating: HE does not want parents to favor one child over another, nor does GOD favor one race over another. Abraham had the same problem when he favored Isaac over Ishmael. The feud that resulted between Isaac and Ishmael is still going on.

These examples from Genesis and Exodus are allegorical. GOD used them to demonstrate HIS will. The GOD I know does not kill HIS children; we (people) through sin, remove GOD'S protection and suffer the consequences.

SEVEN

"But go on now to the end of your life and your rest; for you will

rise again and have your full share of those last days." (Daniel 12:13 TLB)

Daniel after his life on Earth returns to the HOLY SPIRIT for a period of rest. He then returns to Earth in the last days of an age. I doubt that the end of the age is the end of the Earth but rather an awakening to the reality of the HOLY SPIRIT. The awakening also includes the realization that Heaven exists here and now on Earth. It is up to people to realize what the HOLY SPIRIT was telling us in Genesis and Exodus and JESUS/GOD with: ***What you bind on Earth is bound in Heaven and what you loose on Earth is loosed in Heaven!***

NEW TESTAMENT
ONE

Paul stayed in the city several days after that and then said good-bye to the Christians and sailed for the coast of Syria, taking Priscilla and Aquila with him. At Cenchrea, Paul had his head shaved according to Jewish custom, for he had taken a vow. (Acts 18:18 TLB)

So Paul agreed to their request and the next day went with the men to the Temple for the ceremony, thus publicizing his vow to offer a sacrifice seven days later with the others. (Acts 21:26-27 TLB)

The commander arrested him and ordered him bound with double chains. Then he asked the crowd who he was and what he had done. (Acts 21:33 TLB)

JESUS had cancelled the Jewish system of worship with his statement and cleansing of the Temple in Luke 19:41-46.

Paul had looked back to Judaism which was equivalent of Lot's wife looking back to Sodom and Gomorrah. Consequently he was arrested and remained under arrest for the rest of his life.

TWO

Your Heavenly FATHER will forgive you if you forgive those who sin against you; but if you refuse to forgive them, HE will not forgive you. (Matthew 6:14-15 TLB)

We set our own standards, if they are low we, our associates and descendents will suffer. If our level is in accordance with the HOLY SPIRIT'S plans we enter Heaven now on Earth.

THREE

What a terrible thing it is that you are boasting about your purity, and yet you let this sort of thing go on. Don't you realize that if even one person is allowed to go on sinning, soon all will be affected? (1 Corinthians 5:6 TLB)

One member of a congregation can infect others, yes infect!

FOUR

"Don't imagine that I came to bring peace to Earth! No, rather a sword. I have come to set a man against his father, and a daughter against her mother, and a daughter-in-law against her mother-in-law—a man's worst enemies will be right in his own home! If you love your father and mother more than you love ME, you are not worthy of being MINE; or if you love your son or daughter more than ME, you are not worthy of being MINE. If you refuse to take up your cross and follow ME, you are not worthy of being MINE. If you cling to your life, you will lose it; but if you give it up for ME, you will save it." (Matthew 10:34-39 TLB)

We must separate our self from sinners. You will need all the power of the HOLY SPIRIT to do so within families and keep a peaceful relationship.

GOSPEL OF THOMAS

ONE

JESUS said,"People think, perhaps, that I have come to throw peace upon the world. They don't know that I have come to throw disagreement upon the world, and fire, and sword, and struggle. For there will be five in one house. Three will oppose two. Two will oppose three. The father will oppose his son and the son oppose his father. And they will stand up and they will be alone." (16)

We must oppose sin. There is no quick and easy answer as to how each person or family will handle this situation, each must rely on the HOLY SPIRIT.

TWO

If you do not fast from the world you will not find the Kingdom. If you do not keep the Sabbath as a Sabbath you will never see the FATHER. (27)

If we continue to live as the world lives we will not enter the Garden of Eden, which is Heaven on Earth. The only Heaven is for this lifetime on this Earth. See the last verse in Daniel 12:31.

We must limit social contact with sinners. The Sabbath as established in Genesis is the correct day, not what Emperor Constantine recommended.

SHEPHERD OF HERMAS

ONE

He said to me; "Be sincere and be innocent, and you will be like little children who do not know the evil that destroys the life of man. First, speak evil of no one, and do not enjoy listening to someone who does. Otherwise you, the listener, will be responsible for the sin of the one speaking evil, if you believe the

slander which you have heard, for by believing it you yourself will hold a grudge against your brother. In this way you will become responsible for the sin of the one who speaks the evil."
(Hermas 27:1-2)

TWO

"I command you," he said, "to guard purity, and let no thought enter your heart about another man's wife or about fornication, or about some such similar evil thing, for in doing this you commit a major sin. But always keep your mind on your own wife and you will never go wrong. For if this desire enters your heart, you will go wrong, and if other things as evil as this enter, you commit sin. For this desire in a servant of GOD is a major sin, and if anyone does this evil deed, he brings death on himself. So beware; have nothing to do with this desire; for where Holiness lives, there lawlessness ought not to enter the heart of a righteous man."

I said to him, "Sir, allow me to ask you a few questions."

"Speak," he replied.

"Sir," I said, "if a man has a wife who believes in the LORD, and he finds her in some adulterous situation, does the man sin if he continues to live with her?"

"As long as he is unaware of it," he said, "he does not sin. But if the husband knows about her sin and the wife does not repent, but persists in her immorality, and the husband continues to live with her, he becomes responsible for her sin and an accomplice in her adultery."

"So what, sir," I said, "should the husband do, if the wife persists in this passion?"

"Let him divorce her," he said, "and let the husband live by himself. But if after divorcing his wife he should marry another, then he too commits adultery"

"So, then, sir," I said, "if after the wife is divorced, she repents and wants to return to her own husband, she will be taken back, won't she?"

"Certainly," he said. "If the husband does not take her back, he sins, and brings a major sin upon himself. In fact, the one who has sinned and repented must be taken back. But not repeatedly: for there is only one repentance for GOD'S servants. So, because of the possibility of her repentance, the husband ought not to marry. This procedure applies to wife and husband. Not only," he said, "is it adultery if a man pollutes his flesh, but whoever does anything like what the heathen do commits adultery. So, if anyone persists in actions such as these and does not repent, have nothing to do with him and do not live with him. Otherwise you too are a partner in his sin. This is why you are commanded to remain single, whether husband or wife, for in such cases repentance is possible. I am not," He said, "giving an excuse for this affair to end this way, but so that the sinner should sin no more. As for his previous sin, there is ONE WHO is able to give healing; it is HE WHO has authority over everything." (Hermas 29:1-11)

This is the complete answer for divorce as well as an example of sin by association and forgiveness.

THREE

"I would like to know, sir," I said, "in what ways I must serve the good desire."

"Listen," he said, "Practice righteousness and virtue, truth and fear of the LORD, faith and gentleness, and whatever good things are like these. By practicing these you will be an acceptable servant of GOD and will live to HIM; indeed, all who serve the good desire will live to GOD."

So he finished the twelve commandments, and said to me:

"You have the commandments; walk in them and encourage your listeners, in order that their repentance may be pure the rest of the days of their lives. Carefully execute this ministry which I am giving you and you will accomplish much. For you will find favor with those who are going to repent, and they will obey your words, for I will be with you and will compel them to obey you."

I said to him, "Sir, these commandments are great and good and glorious, and are able to gladden the heart of the man who is able to keep them. But I do not know if these commandments can be kept by man, for they are very hard."

He answered and said to me, "If you propose to yourself that they can be kept, you will keep them easily and they will not be hard. But if the idea that they cannot be kept by man has already entered your heart, you will not keep them. But now I say to you: If you do not keep them, you will not have salvation, nor will your children nor your family, since you have already decided for your self that these commandments cannot be kept by man." (Hermas 46:1-6)

If our motives are right, the HOLY SPIRIT will help us to keep the commandments. However, there are times when HE will test us! We cannot be careless.

The children will have the opportunity to accept JESUS when they come of a responsible age.

The writing known as *The Shepherd of Hermas* closes most of the loopholes mankind has found or created in the New Testament. War is killing and Saturday Sabbath are not covered in *Hermas,* at least I have not encountered them. I highly recommend *Hermas* and *The Gospel of Thomas.*

SECOND SECTION
Ezekiel

January 1974, I was employed, as a flight instructor, at the Stuart, FL airport. One of my students testified to me that she believed in JESUS, also that I should contact Till White a friend of hers. She planned to go north the next day or soon. My reaction, later, was that I had to go to CHURCH the following Sunday. I did. They had communion that Sunday and during the service I mentally said to myself, "LORD forgive me," or "JESUS forgive me." There was no particular sin in mind except, I had not accepted JESUS as reality.

Prior to that time I had JESUS in the same category as fictitious characters. JESUS forgave me instantly. When I left the church, that day, I was floating. All the weight was off my back. The minister asked me, as I was leaving, "Do you accept JESUS as LORD?" I answered, "Yes." My wife and I were in the process of joining his congregation, and the question was part of the application.

The following Wednesday I went to Don & Till White's house. While I was sitting at their breakfast counter, Till told me, "Put your hands up in the air and say, 'Praise the LORD,' seven times." I thought, "How stupid can you get?" But I did, about the fifth 'Praise the LORD' SOMEBODY turned on the lights. Everything became new and extremely brighter. I was filled with complete joy and was in harmony with all of mankind.

I learned later that the SOMEBODY was GOD, JESUS or the HOLY SPIRIT. I was also told later, by a marriage counselor, that I had had a Pentecostal experience. I asked, "What's Pentecost?" The Whites told me about a charismatic prayer group that met on Thursday evenings, which I began attending shortly thereafter. The prayer group was primarily Roman Catholic, with a few Methodists and Episcopalians. There may have been other denominations represented. Denominationalism was not the subject of the meetings, only JESUS. Two Catholic priests attended infrequently, but never with their collars on. I was a regular attendee for five years.

At one of the charismatic prayer meetings, probably in late 1975, Gloria Battey exclaimed, "Somebody read Ezekiel 33." Today I have no idea who the person was that read Ezekiel at the meeting, but SOMEONE did for me. To me, it was GOD talking directly to me. Tears of great joy flowed. I suggest that you read all of Ezekiel 33; I will quote only verses 7 thru 9 here.

"So with you, son of dust, I have appointed you as a watchman for the people of Israel; therefore listen to what I say and warn them for ME. When I say to the wicked, 'O wicked man, you will die!' and you don't tell him what I say, so that he does not repent—that wicked person will die in his sins, but I will hold you responsible for his death. But if you warn him to repent and he doesn't he will die in his sin, and you will not be responsible." (Ezekiel 33:7:9 TLB)

A few days later, I was reading Ezekiel 33 and continued on

into 34. Again, GOD was speaking to me, thru the Bible this time, about chapter 34. I will quote only verses 7 thru 10, but the entire chapter is relevant.

"Therefore, O shepherds, hear the word of the LORD:

"As I live, says the LORD GOD, you abandoned MY flock, leaving them to be attacked and destroyed, and you were no real shepherds at all, for you didn't search for them. You fed your-selves and let them starve, therefore I am against the shepherds, and I will hold them responsible for what has happened to MY flock. I will take away their right to feed the flock—and take away their right to eat. I will save MY flock from being taken for their food." (Ezekiel 34:7-10 TLB)

The first Scripture I became aware of that was being ig-nored by many denominations.

Now there was man of the Pharisees, named Nicodemus, a ruler of the JEWS. This man came to JESUS by night and said to HIM, "Rabbi, we know that you are a teacher come from GOD; for no one can do these signs that YOU do, unless GOD is with HIM." JESUS answered him, "Truly, truly, I say to you, unless one is Born Anew, (Born Again) he cannot see the Kingdom of GOD." Nicodemus said to HIM, "How can a man be born when he is old? Can he enter a second time into his mother's womb and be born?" JESUS answered, "Truly, truly, I say to you, unless one is born of water and the SPIRIT, he cannot enter the Kingdom of GOD. That which is born of the flesh is flesh, and that which is Born of the SPIRIT is SPIRIT. Do not marvel that I said to you, 'You must be Born Anew.' The wind blows where it wills and you hear the sound of it, but you do not know whence it comes or whither it goes; so it is with every one who is born of the SPIRIT." (John 3:1-8 RSV)

The first denominational minister I talked to about my Born Again experience did not want to discus the matter. My mother-in-law reported that the minister said: "Bob is tryng to tell me how to run my CHURCH."

The second minister, different denomination, told me, "When someone gets Born Again in my congregation, I ask them to leave.'"

Not all who see the Kingdom GOD will enter the Kingdom of GOD.

The next major area that is ignored almost 100%.

Then HE left Capernaum and went southward to the Judean borders and into the area east of the Jordan River. And as always there were the crowds; and as usual HE taught them.

Some Pharisees came and asked HIM, "Do you permit divorce?" Of course they were trying to trap HIM.

"What did Moses say about divorce?" JESUS asked them.

"He said it was all right," they replied. "He said that all a man has to do is write his wife a letter of dismissal."

"And why did he say that?" JESUS asked. "I'll tell you why—it was a concession to your hard-hearted wickedness. But it certainly isn't GOD'S way. For from the very first HE made man and woman to be joined together permanently in marriage; therefore a man is to leave his father and mother, and he and his wife are united so that they are no longer two, but one. And no man may separate what GOD has joined together."

Later, when HE was alone with HIS disciples in the house, they brought up the subject again.

HE told them, "When a man divorces his wife to marry someone else, he commits adultery against her. And if a wife divorces her husband and remarries, she, too, commits adultery."

(Mark 10:1-11 TLB)

Third

"Not all who sound religious are really GODLY people. They may refer to ME as 'LORD,' but still won't get to Heaven. For

the decisive question is whether they obey MY FATHER in Heaven. At the Judgment many will tell ME, 'LORD, LORD, we told others about YOU and used YOUR NAME to cast out demons and to do many other great miracles.' But I will reply, 'You have never been MINE. Go away, for your deeds are evil.'" (Matthew 7:21-23 TLB)

Obedience is the primary requirement after accepting JESUS, as LORD.

Fourth

Now at last the heavens and Earth were successfully completed, with all that they contained. So on the seventh day, having finished HIS task, GOD ceased from this work HE had been doing, and GOD blessed the seventh day and declared it Holy, because it was the day when HE ceased this work of creation. (Genesis 2:1`-3 TLB) Constantine issued an edict in March 321 AD changing the Sabbath day to Sunday.

Do we want to follow Emperor Constantine or Genesis 2:1-3?

After this, JESUS knowing that all things were now accomplished that the Scripture might be fulfilled, saith, "I thirst." Now there was set a vessel full of vinegar; and they filled a sponge with vinegar, and put it to HIS mouth. When JESUS therefore had received the vinegar, HE said; "It is finished." And HE bowed HIS head, and gave up the GHOST. (John 19:28-30 KJV)

JESUS finished HIS work on the sixth day, rested (slept) the seventh day and rose on the first day of the week.

Fifth

Then the Pharisees met together to try to think of some way to trap JESUS into saying something for which they could arrest HIM. They decided to send some of their men along with the Herodians to ask HIM this question: "SIR, we know YOU are very honest and teach the truth regardless of the consequences, without fear or favor. Now tell us, is it right to pay taxes to the Roman government or not?"

But JESUS saw what they were after. "You hypocrites!" HE exclaimed. "Who are you trying to fool with your trick questions? Here, show ME a coin." And they handed HIM a penny.

"Whose picture is stamped on it?" HE asked them. "And whose name is this beneath the picture?"

"Caesar's," they replied.

"Well, then," HE said, "give it to Caesar if it is his, and give GOD everything that belongs to GOD." (Matthew 22:15-21 TLB)

We are to support the government with our tax money and we are to give to the poor as JESUS described in Matthew 19:21 and Matthew 25:31—46. We owe obedience to our CREATOR.

Sixth

And we know that all that happens to us is working for our good if we love GOD and are fitting into HIS plans. (Romans 8:28 TLB)

Are we fitting into GOD'S plans?

PRAYER & TRAFFIC PATTERN

But seek first the Kingdom of GOD and HIS righteousness, and all these things shall be added to you. (Matthew 6:33 NKJV)

GOD'S righteousness starts with us accepting; 'JESUS CHRIST died for us, while we were yet sinners.' Then we must obey HIM, that we might be filled with HIS HOLY SPIRIT, John 14:15-16. In event of disobedience see the 4th chapter of Matthew, which describes how Satan can deceive us. The CHURCH leaders were deceived when they changed the Sabbath and claimed they could annul marriages.

And in the same way—by our faith—the HOLY SPIRIT helps us with our daily problems and in our praying. For we don't even know what we should pray for, nor how to pray as we should; but the HOLY SPIRIT prays for us with such feeling that it cannot be expressed in words. And the FATHER WHO knows all hearts knows, of course, what the SPIRIT is saying as HE pleads for us in harmony with GOD'S own will. And we know that all that happens to us is working for our good if we love GOD and are fitting into HIS plans. (Romans 8:26-28 TLB)

To me, these three verses represent our daily life as well as looking forward to the Day of Judgment. JESUS tells us in Matthew 7:21; if we want a good report of Judgment Day, we must have been obedient to our FATHER in Heaven. The choice is our own to make.

Allow me to tell you about a series of events, of many, that GOD led me thru; to demonstrate HIS power or the power of the HOLY SPIRIT. GOD, JESUS and the HOLY SPIRIT are ONE!

I was teaching people to fly, at the Stuart, FL airport, from 1973 thru 1987. I had worked for the fixed base operator for about a year and then opened my own business. After opening my business I had to go to Fort Pierce or elsewhere to get gas for my airplanes. It was during this period that my students were having a problem entering the traffic pattern properly, for landing. Their other flying was going fine. I had been teaching flying about 10 years, at this time, and it was the first time I had encountered this problem.

My Born Again experience had occurred in January 1974, the problem existed after that, but before a control tower was put in operation at Stuart. I was quite sure that it was a spiritual problem, as GOD was working in my life in other areas, but I had no idea what the root problem was. When I read from Isaiah 1:22 the solution was made very clear. *"Your silver has become dross, your wine mixed with water."* I could not effectively teach what I did not practice. On trips to Fort Pierce I was cutting corners in the traffic pattern. The law states that, "All turns shall be to left, unless otherwise designated, as you approach for a landing at an airport without a control tower." In order to save time, which is money in an airplane, I was not following the recommended procedure in the Flight Information Manual. I knew that going straight in for a landing was hazardous, but that is what I was doing, when I was alone in the plane. The recommended pattern consists of downwind leg parallel to the runway with a base leg 90 degrees to the runway and then straight in for landing. On each leg the wings need to be level for a time, to be able to check for other planes.

I resolved to quit cutting corners and did. I had done nothing illegal, but was not following proper procedure. Nor was I doing what I was teaching the students. Shortly thereafter I had three near misses, on which the HOLY SPIRIT warned me, preventing an accident.

The first was on a landing at the Okeechobee airport. I had picked up a passenger at Indiantown and was to pick up another at Okeechobee. As we approached the Okeechobee airport I knew something was wrong, similar to intuition, but much stronger. I received a landing advisory from UNICOM, entered the pattern properly; all the while being very cautious. There was very little wind; planes could be using any runway. After touching down on the runway, another plane landed on the same runway, only at the other end.

Second event: A student and I were on the way to Fort

Pierce, from Stuart. We were flying legally, below a layer of clouds. Again the premonition, something is wrong. I had the student make a slight left turn, continuing on toward Fort Pierce. Shortly, after the turn, a business jet came out of the bottom of the clouds, just off our right wing. He may have seen us or we may have been on radar, I don't know, but it would have been too close if we had not turned left. The jet pilot was also on his way to Fort Pierce.

Third: I was doing practice takeoffs and landings with a student at Stuart. Premonition; something wrong, much stronger than the previous warnings. The student was flying and doing fine. As we were on the final leg to land, I grabbed the flight controls and turned to the right very abruptly. I had seen nothing wrong, nor was I instructed to turn right, it was something I just did. It turned out to be the move that saved our lives. Just as we banked for the right turn, I caught a glimpse of another plane diving thru the path we had just vacated.

In these events each step was closer to an accident than the previous event. Had there only been one or two I would have dismissed them as coincidence but the third near miss made a believer of me, that GOD was in control, but only if I live according to HIS will. Because of the sacrifice, by JESUS we are forgiven when we repent. My students were being affected because of my actions, which they knew nothing of. Matthew 18:18 is TRUTH. *What we bind on Earth is bound in Heaven and what we lose on Earth is loosed in Heaven!!*

ISAAC

Later on, GOD tested Abraham's (faith and obedience).
   "Abraham!" GOD called.
   "Yes, LORD?" he replied.

"*Take with you your only son—yes, Isaac whom you love so much—and go to the land of Moriah and sacrifice him there as a burnt offering upon one of the mountains which I'll point out to you!*"

The next morning Abraham got up early, chopped wood for a fire upon the altar, saddled his donkey, and took with him his son Isaac and two young men who were his servants, and started off to the place where GOD had told him to go. On the third day of the journey Abraham saw the place in the distance.

"*Stay here with the donkey,*" Abraham told the young men, "*and the lad and I will travel yonder and worship, and then come right back.*"

Abraham placed the wood for the burnt offering upon Isaac's shoulders, while he himself carried the knife and the flint for striking a fire. So the two of them went on together.

"*Father,*" Isaac asked, "*we have the wood and the flint to make the fire, but where is the lamb for the sacrifice?*"

"*GOD will see to it, my son,*" Abraham replied. And they went on.

When they arrived at the place where GOD had told Abraham to go, he built an altar and placed the wood in order, ready for the fire, and then tied Isaac and laid him on the altar over the wood. And Abraham took the knife and lifted it up to plunge it into his son, to slay him.

At that moment the Angel of GOD shouted to him from Heaven, "*Abraham! Abraham!*"

"*Yes, LORD!*" he answered.

"*Lay down the knife; don't hurt the lad in any way,*" the Angel said, "*for I know that GOD is first in your life—you have not withheld even your beloved son from ME.*"

Then Abraham noticed a ram caught by its horns in a bush. So he took the ram and sacrificed it, instead of his son, as a burnt *offering on the altar. Abraham named the place "JEHOVAH provides"—and it still goes by that name to this day.*

Then the Angel of GOD called again to Abraham from Heaven. "I, the LORD, have sworn by MYSELF that because you have obeyed ME and have not withheld even your beloved son from ME, I will bless you with incredible blessings and multiply your descendants into countless thousands and million, like the stars above you in the sky, and like the sands along the seashore. These descendants of yours will conquer their enemies, and be a blessing to all the nations of the Earth—all because you have obeyed ME."

(Genesis 22:1-18 TLB)

In 1974 I received a $20,000 advance on my share of my father's estate, to start a flight school at Stuart. The first plane I purchased was a Cessna 150, paid for it in full and then later purchased a Grumman American Traveler. The Traveler was financed and at the time I signed the contract, for the Traveler, I wrote on the contract, "I would get it paid for with GOD'S help." See my testimony under TITHE for details on the Traveler.

Later, I borrowed $2,000 from First National Bank, Stuart, using the Cessna as collateral. I was reluctant to borrow money against the Cessna. It was only at the HOLY SPIRIT'S urging, "Borrow money," that I did borrow the $2,000.

"And if, as MY representatives, you give even a cup of cold water to a little child, you will surely be rewarded." (Matthew 10:42 TLB)

GOD had been meeting my financial needs for sometime because I relied on Matthew 10:42. I would do a good deed for someone and the money would come in. I had received the message to borrow money several times, but to me that was only going to make the financial situation worse. I checked with First National bank for a loan but was told they did not loan money on airplanes. One of my early students had agreed to loan me the $2,000. He phoned, one day, and said he could not loan me the money, Terry Keathly was in the office at the time of the call. When he learned what had happened he called First National Bank and told them to loan me the money even if had to co-sign. The bank then made the loan but Terry did not co-sign.

At this same time I was being urged to name the airplane 'Isaac.' I talked a local minister into painting the name Isaac on the plane in exchange for a plane ride. I knew GOD was setting me up for something; it was my job to trust HIM. Yes, I was reading Genesis 22, several times, during these proceedings.

Sure enough, I got behind on payments to the bank. I had met with the collection officer several times and at one meeting, I blurted out, "You set the deadline and GOD will give me the money." At the deadline I had $200, but owed about $1,000. I gave them the choice the $200 or the plane, they took the $200. But soon they set another deadline.

On the day of the second deadline, Bill Carrasco was to come to the office for ground instruction at 1 PM. The collection officer had given me his after hours phone number and said to call him by 5 PM. Bill called and said he was waiting on a phone call and would come as soon as he could, but he would not be there at 1 PM. Bill arrived about 3 PM. Bill knew I was having money problems, but knew nothing of the deadline or the amount involved. At five minutes to five, Bill stood up and was dancing a jig, as though the floor was hot. He pulled out a check and said he had to give it to me. I called the collection officer and he said to bring the money in the next day. Bill offered to have the check endorsed by his employer, but I said, "No, this is the way GOD gave it and it was the way I was to take it to the bank."

The check was written in Spanish on a Porto Rican bank, made out to "Cash." Dated 23 Feb '77. It was not endorsed.

When the people at the bank saw the check, they didn't laugh, but they certainly informed me the check was not to be honored. The best they could do would be to send it thru channels and see if it was honored, but in the meantime I needed about $1,200.

I ended up in a vice-president's office, I think his name was Jim Mitchell, he explained the banking laws for about the third time that morning. Eventually he was called from his office. I sat there praying in tongues and asking GOD, "I'm here with your check, what now?" I hear, ***"Ask them, 'What would happen if Evans Crary put is name on the back of it?'"***

Mr. Mitchell called Evans' office to see if he was in. He was there, so I took the check upstairs to Evans' office and waited in his waiting room. After a short wait Evans stuck his head out of the door and asked what he could do for me. I asked, "Would you endorse this for me?" He endorsed it without looking at the check. I went back downstairs with a handful of gold, worth gold anyway. The bank got paid and I had enough left to pay Fort Pierce Flying Service for an inspection they were doing on the plane.

After settling with the bank, I went back to Evans' office to thank him. It was noon now. When Evans came out of his office, the first words I heard were, "Bob, where did that check come from?"

I answered, "GOD." That was not what Evans wanted to hear and the conversation ended rather abruptly.

TITHE

"If I were hungry, I would not mention it to you—for all the world is MINE, and everything in it. No I don't need your sacrifices of flesh and blood. What I want from you is your true thanks: I want your promises fulfilled. I want you to trust ME in your times of trouble, so I can rescue you, and you can give ME glory." (Psalm 50:12-15 TLB)

When I first started reading the Bible, after my conversion, I had read it 2 or 3 times; from cover to cover and then, this was the first verse I marked. I believed it summarized GOD'S intent for our lives. I have never assumed that it meant we should not tithe, but that morality was more important, and to trust HIM in our times of trouble.

"And I will give you the keys of the Kingdom of Heaven; whatever doors you lock on Earth shall be locked in Heaven; and whatever doors you open on Earth shall be open in Heaven." (Matthew 16:19 TLB)

When we take these two passages together, GOD is giving us (all people) the responsibility for why and how HE will intervene in our lives as well as the responsibility for a good report, by JESUS on Judgment Day. JESUS came to demonstrate the true nature of GOD. JESUS' instructions in the New Testament are how HE expects us to live, that HE might rescue us, including the basis for HIS final Judgment. JESUS also gives us an opportunity to repent, when we realize we have made a mistake.

Yes, woe upon you, Pharisees, and you other religious leaders—hypocrites!! For you tithe down to the last mint leaf in your garden, but ignore the important things—justice and mercy and faith. Yes, you should tithe, but you shouldn't leave the more important things undone. Blind guides! You strain out a gnat and swallow a camel." (Matthew 23:23-24 TLB)

These two verses support the first two passages, I quoted.

If our motives are right, GOD might ask us to do something that goes against our normal actions. HE will communicate with us directly; JESUS is our HIGH PRIEST (Hebrews 8:1). If motives are wrong we will end up following Satan, see the fourth chapter of Matthew. We must seek a relationship with GOD, JESUS, and the HOLY SPIRIT, alone; not for financial or prestigious reward. Love GOD with all your heart, mind and soul.

When I first started a flight school at Stuart my intention was to obtain a fixed base operation on the airport. It became apparent that it was not GOD'S will for me to be a fixed base operator: I first used the Cessna (Isaac) to pay the Fort Pierce Flying Service account and then was looking for a buyer for the Traveler. I went to see Duke; he had expressed an interest in buying an airplane. After visiting with him a while; he said he was not interested in buying the plane, but he would make the payments and I could keep the plane. That is what we did.

A few months later I received a notice, from the finance company, the payments were not being made. That evening I attended a lecture by a Jewish Christian, who was teaching on the Covenants of GOD. At the close of the meeting he announced. "There is someone here who is not keeping his tithe, and GOD is not able to free up the money." There was no doubt, he was referring to me. Duke had moved from Florida, where? I didn't know. Later found out he was in Arizona.

I had been making out IOUs for my tithe because I was short of money. I went to my office to look at my finances. There was not enough money, combined in the company account and my personal account to cover the tithe. But I was being urged, by the HOLY SPIRIT, to cover the tithe. I finally wrote a check on my business account for wages and then used a personal check for the tithe. The business account would be overdrawn, but I assumed the check for office rent would probably not be in. The office owner was expected to be in California for a week; giving me time to cover the business account. The check for office rent had been given to his secretary, but the checks usually, were not deposited in his absence. I knew that overdrawing a checking account was not a solution for my financial problems, but that is what I was getting from the HOLY SPIRIT.

A few weeks later, I received notice from the finance company, the payments have been resumed.

Today, I still wonder if I would have overdrawn the account if I had not known that the office owner was out of town. None of the checks bounced.

MOSES AND ROCKS

And HE said to Moses, "Get Aaron's rod; then you and Aaron must summon the people. As they watch, speak to that rock over there and tell it to pour out its water! You will give them water from a rock, enough for all the people and all their cattle!"

So Moses did as instructed. He took the rod from the place where it was kept before the LORD; then Moses and Aaron summoned the people to come and gather at the rock; and he said to them, "Listen, you rebels: Must we bring you water from this rock?"

Then Moses lifted the rod and struck the rock twice, and water gushed out; and the people and their cattle drank.

But the LORD said to Moses and Aaron, "Because you did not believe ME and did not sanctify ME you shall not bring them into the land I have promised them!"

This place was named Meribah, meaning 'Rebel Waters',

because it was where the people of Israel fought against JEHOVAH, and where HE showed HIMSELF to be Holy before them. (Numbers 20:7-13 TLB)

GOD had impressed this passage on me, while I still owned the Cessna. The radio in the Cessna had problems. I mean it had bad problems. At first I had the radio repaired in Fort Lauderdale. Then later a radio shop opened in Fort Pierce and I had the work done there. The radio had been in the Fort Pierce shop for weeks. The shop owner and his technician were telling me two different stories, as to what was wrong with the radio. Frustrating to say the least. They finally agreed that the radio needed a 'synthesizer.' They did not have a synthesizer, nor were they able to get one, so they said. I was sure that the radio shop in Fort Lauderdale had a synthesizer; as they had replaced it before.

My inclination was to take the radio to Fort Lauderdale and tell the radio shop owner, in Fort Pierce, what I thought of him. The HOLY SPIRIT was continually prompting me to be patient, not to hit the rock as Moses had done, when they needed water. I was to practice what JESUS had taught in the Beatitudes. The same principle JESUS had given HIS disciples when HE sent out the disciples with HIS message. If the people did not accept the message they were to shake the dust off their feet and leave. Demonstrate no anger.

I had told a friend, Big Ed, the saga of the radio. Then one day, Big Ed and I were visiting, when the HOLY SPIRIT prompted me to call the radio shop in Fort Pierce and ask about the radio. The shop owner said he had just received notice that the synthesizer had been shipped from Wichita, KS. Big Ed and I went to lunch. When I returned to the office, I was informed the radio shop owner had phoned, "The radio is ready, you can pick it up anytime."

The shop owner said the delivery man walked thru his door with the parts just as he hung up the phone after talking to me. Later, he mentioned the unusual sequence, of his receiving notice of shipment, my call and delivery of the parts, they followed each other immediately.

For years, I thought the two main messages taught in Numbers 20:7-13 were, to obey GOD exactly as HE said and to control anger. GOD was also reminding me that HE can control the timing of events, and not to exaggerate.

A couple of years later, someone paid for a trip to the Holy Land and gave it to Big Ed. He visited the well that Moses had struck and he brought me a small rock from the well.

After, I was Born Again; GOD controlled the timing in my life, for many months. If I was early or late for an appointment the other party was also early or late. The phone never rang when I was busy; it rang when I had finished a task. I could drive thru Fort Pierce and not have to stop at a traffic light except the last one or two. I could make out a flight navigation log and all the check point times were exact except the last one or two. I had told others of this timing, but said I could go all the way thru Fort Pierce without a stop or complete a flight with all the times exact. The HOLY SPIRIT stopped me from exaggerating, HE informed me that if HE had made all the times perfect, I would become careless.

Recently, 1997, I was telling a friend about Moses and the rock and the timing when the HOLY SPIRIT abruptly informed me that GOD did not need HIS deeds to be exaggerated, HE would provide the material, as needed

FOUR DREAMS

For some time I have been very much aware that we live in a

spiritual world. I have decided: I only want to have something to do with that which is represented by JESUS.

Three of the dreams have meaning only in the fact that the future was revealed to me. They do not denote right or wrong, just events accurately depicted. The fourth dream, or vision, is an accurate interpretation of Mark 10:1-12; Matthew 5:31-32; Matthew 19:1-12 and Luke 16:18. JESUS is giving us a definition of adultery that most people do not accept. The fourth dream also showed me what the results would be, in the future, if I continued on course of action I was then on.

The first dream occurred, on a Sunday night, during the mid 1960s. I was at NAS Glenview, IL, just outside Chicago, for a weekend drill. I was in the Navy Reserve. I was going for a job interview with the Service Department of Ford Motor Co., in Chicago on Monday. In the dream, I saw a large room divided by glass partitions for work stations. The manager's section was fully enclosed. The receptionist and others I was introduced to were remembered. There was a glass coffee table in the manager's office. When I went to the Ford interview nothing was the same, I was disappointed. However, a few months later I talked to a personnel manager, at Volkswagen, and it was exactly the same as the dream.

The second dream occurred 19 January 1969, at Lajes, Azores, after a flight from Argentia, Newfoundland. We were on the way to Rota, Spain for our two weeks annual active duty. On arriving at Lajes some of the crew went to eat, others of us decided to go to bed, it was late. I dreamt that I walked across the road and thru the door to the mess hall. Once thru the door there was a foyer, steps going down and then a wide hall with chairs, end tables, lamps and carpet. Not the usual military mess hall. When I got up the next morning I was convinced, in my mind, that I had eaten the night before. However when I went to breakfast and saw the mess hall I realized that it had been a dream. It was in January 1974 that I visited a restaurant in Florida and saw what I had seen in the dream.

The third event dream would have occurred in the mid 1980s. In the dream I was driving north on a road in Stuart, FL, turned and went east to a certain street, then north and stopped. I walked up a lane to a house and then the dream ended. I did not know why I went to the house. I was familiar with the street where the dream started, but not the side streets. A few days later I drove over the route, to see if I could figure out what was going on. In May 1990 the dream was fulfilled. As I drove north, on the street where the dream started, about a block, before turning east I realized I was in the vehicle in the dream. I took a newspaper to the house that was in the dream. My job, then, was as Service Assistant for the Palm Beach Newspaper, which consisted of taking a paper to customers that had been missed by the carrier. I had stopped to write down the address where the dream began. The office would call me on a two way radio with the addresses.

The only one I know, who can give foreknowledge, is GOD.

The fourth dream or vision is different in message content but in the reality of the dream it is the same. When I awake I am as aware of the event as though it had actually taken place.

The fourth dream occurred in late December 1979. I dreamt: JESUS was lying on the Cross on the ground and I was putting a nail in HIS left wrist. When I stood up and turned around, HE was standing there. HE handed me a handful of nails. Nothing was said but I knew that I could pass out the nails to others so they could also nail HIM to the Cross. I had plenty of nails to continue nailing HIM to the Cross myself.

The event I had participated in that nailed JESUS to the Cross was a second marriage. JESUS was showing me that I was a sinner. My first marriage ended in a divorce in 1975. I was then married the second time 15 December 1979. I repented, which meant another divorce to comply with the law of the land, but from GOD'S viewpoint I was not married the second time. JESUS defined it as adultery.

I was setting an example, to others, it was OK to divorce my original wife, and then remarry someone else. There is a passage from *The Shepherd of Hermas* which is applicable to our keeping GOD'S commandments.

I (Hermas) said to him, "Sir, these commandments age great and good and glorious, and are able to gladden the heart of the man who is able to keep them. But I do not know if these commandments can be kept by man, for they are very hard."

He (Angel of Repentance) answered and said to me, "If you propose to yourself that they can be kept, you will keep them easily and they will not be hard. But if the idea that they cannot be kept by man has already entered our heart, you will not keep them. But now I say to you: If you do not keep them, but neglect them, you will not have Salvation, nor will your children nor your family, since you have already decided for yourself that these commandments cannot be kept by man." (Hermas 46:4-6)

Yes, it is important for the parents to provide Salvation for their children, while they are young.

If we were to ask JESUS, today, about divorce we would get the same answer HE gave in Mark 10:1-12.

A PIECE OF PAPER

30 January 1946: On a formation flight from NAS Deland, FL to Fort Lauderdale, in SB2C #20552, the following occurred. As we passed just west of NAS Stuart, the flight leader announced, on the radio, that we were passing NAS Stuart. As I looked at NAS Stuart I heard someone say; *"That is your home."* It was not audible, but very distinct. My reaction was; "That is not my home, I live in Iowa."

In 1973 I was employed as a flight instructor at Stuart. Then operated my own flight school 1974 thru 1985. Sold the airplanes and business in 1985 and then managed the school two years for the new owner.

December 1974: My wife and I had separated. I was renting an apartment in Stuart and praying for GOD to help me find a place I could buy for $1,000 down payment. I was going southwest of Stuart, on Kanner Highway, to look at a mobile home. The left rear wheel cover came off the 1965 Ford I was driving. It had been bent and had a habit of coming off. I would hear it hit the road, go get it and put it back on. Same this time, except now I was asking GOD to help find the wheel cover. Very distinctly, *"You will get a wheel cover with where you are to live."* I got back in the car. A few days later I looked at a mobile home in Ridgeway Mobil Home Park. The sales manager, Mr. Lanham, and I viewed the trailer and had gone back to his office. Terry Keathly, the park owner, was now at the office. I had taught Terry to fly. The trailer had been abandoned by the previous owner. Mr. Lanham proposed that I take over the payments at the bank, pay for skirting on the trailer, and pay the sales tax. Total came to about $1,000. Terry said I would not have to pay the sales tax until the title was cleared and they would put the skirting on in exchange for flight lessons for Mr. Lanham. There were two bank payments due, each about $250. For some reason I didn't say yes, but went back to look at the trailer, wheel covers were not on my mind, but soon were. As I got out of the car, I saw a wheel cover under the trailer; it fit and appeared similar to the others. Yes, I took over the payments and it was home, until 2001. I moved to Iowa in December 2001.

See "Guilty by Association" for the reason of the move.

There was another time I heard this same voice. It is not audible but very distinct. That was when I was sitting in an official's office of the First National Bank and Trust Co. of Stuart. I was trying to pay the bank some past due accounts with a check on a Porto Rican bank made out to "cash" it was not endorsed by anyone. The check was for $1,800 dated 23 February 1977. He had explained, along with others, why they could not honor the check. He was called from the office and I was praying, in tongues, asking GOD: "I'm here with your check, now what?" I hear; ***"Ask them, what would happen if Evans Crary put his name on the back of it."*** When Mr. Mitchell came back, I asked. Mr. Mitchell said, "Do you suppose Evans would do that?" He called Mr. Crary's office to see if he was in. Evans was there, so I went to his office, which was on the second floor of the bank building. Evans did endorse the check.

(Also in "Isaac")

Patricia and I were divorced in July 1975….I don't have a record. After the divorce, I received the final papers and was about to put them in a file, when I heard: ***"All you have is a piece of paper."*** I threw the piece of paper away. From GOD'S viewpoint; I was never divorced. ***"Let no man put asunder."*** Patricia and I never did reconcile. She passed away in 1987. She had insisted on being cremated, but had consented to me bringing the ashes to the family cemetery plot, in Iowa.

GUILTY BY ASSOCIATION

In March 1991 the Palm Beach Post newspaper ran an editorial titled, "Kids need good homes; some are gay homes." This was the editorial policy of the newspaper. They were supporting homosexuals. I was employed by them as Service Assistant. There was no way the HOLY SPIRIT was going to allow me to work for them, I had no peace. I wrote a letter in opposition to their position. They did not publish it. After a few weeks, I phoned the newspaper and talked to a junior editor. He agreed with me in principle and agreed to talk to his superiors. After a few days I called him back and he said, the newspaper stood firm on the policy of supporting gay rights. However he did agree to have my letter published. The following is my letter as they published it, it had been edited.

This letter is prompted by your suggestion that gay men and women should be allowed to adopt children. I take strong opposition to your position. The family is an important segment of GOD'S order.

Homosexuals are sinning, according to GOD. The Bible teaches the same. Gays are in direct conflict with GOD'S instructions. Children who are raised in this environment are likely to accept it as normal, even though they may not become gay themselves. Others will also be influenced that the gay lifestyle is acceptable.

JESUS CHRIST said, "Then give the emperor all that is his—and give to GOD all that is HIS!" When we support the breakdown of GOD'S normal family, we are not giving GOD that which is HIS. The family is GOD'S creation. The government, which is separate from the CHURCH, may have laws allowing homosexuality, but do not involve innocent children in sin.

Even after my editorial was published, I had no peace. I

told my superior that I was quitting, I could leave then or up to a month later; the choice was his. He opted for the month. My peace came back, as soon as the decision was made.

"Don't imagine that I came to bring peace to the Earth! No, rather, a sword. I have come to set a man against his father, and a daughter against her mother, and a daughter-in-law against her mother-in-law—a man's worst enemies will be right in his own home! If you love father and mother more than you love ME, you are not worthy of being MINE; or if you love your son or daughter more than ME, you are worthy of being MINE. If you refuse to take up your cross and follow ME, you are not worthy of being MINE.

"If you cling to your life, you will lose it; but if you give it up for ME, you will save it." (Matthew 10:34-39 TLB)

Why I moved from the trailer. In March 2001, on the way from Iowa to Florida, I was praising the LORD and mentioned, "JESUS we will soon be home to 7941 Skylark Ave."

After a long pause, JESUS told me, *"I won't live there."* The voice I heard was not the usual clear distinct voice. This voice was a man's voice which sounded half asleep, as though he had just been awakened.

Ridgeway Mobile Home Park does not allow children to live in it. This had always bothered me but I was sure that was where GOD wanted me to live. After receiving the message that JESUS would not live there, I had the trailer torn down and hauled to the dump. If I could have had the lot rolled up and hauled too I would have. In December 2001 I listed the lot for sale and it was sold that summer.

JESUS had always proclaimed; *"Allow the children to come to HIM."*

GOD had provided a place for me to live, when I needed it. When the time was right, I was to move on.

"Flee for your lives," the angels told him. (Lot) "And don't look back. Escape to the mountains. Don't stay down here on the plain or you will die." (Genesis 19:17 TLB)

See chapters 18 & 19 of Genesis for the story of Lot in Sodom and Gomorrah.

GOD SPOKE

The following is my testimony of conversations with GOD. The voice I heard was audible.

One evening, in 1989, I was praising GOD and thanking HIM for the things HE was doing in my life. I also thanked HIM for allowing me to go into the Navy, before HE entered my life, and fly all those great airplanes: Helldiver, Corsair, Bearcat, Cougar, Neptune and others. GOD very abruptly said; *"I didn't send you to the Navy to fly airplanes, I sent you, to learn discipline, which you can't learn in the CHURCH today."* Nothing more was said.

Since then I have reflected on just what discipline HE was talking about. Certainly that we must be punctual, proper uniform, respect authority, and obey orders and commands. The Navy has a tradition. If your Commanding Officer wanted or wished something, you were to comply as though it was an order. During my two tours as a Commanding Officer; I found the greatest problem was with those who were looking for loopholes. I could never depend on them to carry out my intentions. Removing them from positions of responsibility was the usual remedy.

I have attempted to apply, this principle, to carry out GOD'S wishes, as though they were commandments, since my conversion. I am not claiming to be perfect, just trying in my way, to do what GOD wants. I am Saved only by the Grace of GOD, thru JESUS CHRIST. I must repent when

38

I sin, that includes stop doing that which is wrong as well as admitting sorrow for having done wrong.

One of GOD'S commandments is: "Do not commit adultery." JESUS then gave us one definition of adultery. If you get a divorce and marry someone else, it is adultery.

A lot of people think HE also provided some avenues to bypass HIS intent.

Mandate the Fourth from *The Shepherd of Hermas* begins with:

I charge thee,' saith he, 'to keep purity, and let not a thought enter into thy heart concerning another's wife, or concerning fornication, or concerning any such like evil deeds; for in so doing thou committeth a great sin.'

This quote from *Hermas* summarizes GOD'S intent quite well.

In March 1977, I had this conversation with GOD, while standing near the center of the Stuart airport. I had just gotten out of the airplane to watch a student pilot go on his second solo flight.

I heard; ***"You are going to do MY will."***

I said, "Hallelujah, I have been wanting to do that."

HE said, ***"Forget Jane."*** Jane is not her real name, as she does not want it used.

"All right...do I get to get married?"

"For a short time it will be as though you are married."

That was all.

In September of 1975 the following conversation occurred. I was in bed awake, when I heard a voice say, ***"Bobbie, Bobbie."*** I had read Isaiah 45 a few days before and was thinking about Cyrus. There seemed to be a fleeting connection with Cyrus.

My reply, "Yes, LORD."

"I am going to do a great work thru you."

My answer, "I do not want anyone hurt." There was no response.

LIGHTNING

A short time after moving into the trailer, Patricia was coming down for a date. We were still married and both seemed to want to try and repair the marriage. The morning of the day she was to come, I got up full of righteous anger. I was going to make our marriage work. It happened while I was dressing: A bolt of lightning ran across the ceiling on the south side of the bedroom. I not only saw the lightning, I also heard the crackling. The lightning lasted long enough for me to turn and my eyes to focus on it. I looked for a natural cause, knowing that I was not going to find a short in the electrical system. GOD had my attention, but good. I went to the Bible.

But if the unbelieving depart, let him depart. A brother or a sister is not under bondage in such cases; but GOD hath called us to peace. (1 Corinthians 7:15 KJV)

That evening, when Patricia came, I told her I was going to stay in Stuart and if she wanted to come live in the trailer, I would try to reconcile our differences. She did not accept my offer. We were divorced in July 1975. I had found a loophole.

In hindsight, Mark 10:9 prevails over 1 Corinthians 7:15.

"Therefore what GOD has joined together, let not man separate." (Mark 10:9 NKJV)

The second lightning occurred in February 1976. I was reading a book, *The Great Controversy* by Ellen White. In the book the author referred to this Bible passage.

But as they came closer to Jerusalem and HE saw the city ahead, HE began to cry. "Eternal Peace was within your reach and you turned it down," HE wept, "and now it is too late. Your enemies will pile up earth against your walls and encircle you and close in on you, and crush you to the ground, and your children within you; your enemies will not leave one stone upon another—for you have rejected the opportunity GOD offered you." (Luke 19:41-44 TLB)

This Scripture made quite an impression on me. I telephoned a friend to share the Scripture. Just as she answered the phone, lightning occurred across the vacant lot south of the trailer. The lightning was horizontal and not between any known objects. The weather was clear and it was night. To me GOD was saying; *"Pay attention to this Scripture."*

PAY ATTENTION TO THIS SCRIPTURE

When President Bush had the American armies invade Iraq was the fulfillment of *"Pay attention to this Scripture."* This was March 2003.

I became acutely aware that this was the occasion that I had been alerted for. There was, and still is no doubt, in my mind that America is in the same situation that Israel (Jerusalem) was in when JESUS made the proclamation ending the Promised Land Contract.

The situation affected me mentally to the point that I had a case of the 'shingles.' I am taking Paxil (generic) and Protonix still today. (4 November 2006)

Not by might, nor by power, but by MY SPIRIT, saith the LORD OF HOSTS. (Zechariah 4:6b KJV)

President Bush evidently was not aware of this verse, or the following verse.

For the eyes of the LORD run to and fro throughout the whole Earth, to shew HIMSELF strong in the behalf of them whose heart is perfect toward HIM. Herein thou hast done foolishly: therefore from henceforth thou shalt have wars. (2 Chronicles 16:9 KJV)

2 Chronicles 16:9 is an excellent example of the fulfillment of Matthew 18:18 & 16:19

America is on the verge of receiving the same type of prophecy. Bob

MANKIND CONTROLS HIS FUTURE

Several years ago, I was reading the Book of Revelation when I heard: *"Mankind controls his future."*

I took this to mean that Revelation was a man's imagination. When we consider Matthew 18:18 correctly man/woman control the future through the HOLY SPIRIT. Each person has the same potential as JESUS.

"The truth is, anyone who believes in ME will do the same works I have done, and even greater works, because I am going to be with the FATHER." (John 14:12 NLT)

THERE'S NOTHING OUT THERE

While I lived in Florida I went to the Space Center several times. It was fascinating to me. On one of the early trips the HOLY SPIRIT was flat. Then later on a trip I got the message mentally; *"There's nothing out there."*

I assume there is not life elsewhere in the universe. Still the study of the Universe fascinates me. However, I am sure the CREATOR would be more pleased if we spent the money helping the poor of the world.

WELCOME HOME, PARTNER

In December 2000, I was visiting with a friend in New Sharon when I said, "I expect to be back sometime in next February." I had not planned to say this nor had I any plans for being back to New Sharon in February. I left for Florida soon thereafter.

At that time I still had my home in Florida during the winter and came to Iowa for the summer months. Some accused me of being a reverse 'snowbird.'

About the middle of February, while in Florida, the idea kept coming back that I was to keep my word and go to New Sharon in February. I kept putting off going to Iowa, and the intuition or warning kept coming too. Finally, I just left Florida, but did not get to Iowa until early March. The LORD was especially close on the trip to Iowa, while in Iowa and on the return trip to Florida.

I stopped at the first rest stop on the Interstate Highway after arriving in Iowa and as the car came to a stop I heard. ***"Welcome home partner."***

I speculate, a lot, on just what this means but am pleased with it.

While in Iowa the HOLY SPIRIT informed me that my wife was Dottie, the lady I was engaged to. I located her and we exchanged letters and phone calls for a few weeks until she said; "Get lost." Or words to that effect.

I stayed in Iowa about a week and on the return trip to Florida is when JESUS informed me that HE would not live at 7941 Skylark Ave. I reported this under 'Guilty by Association' above.

In October 2001 while mowing grass, with a riding lawn-mower, I was anointed by the HOLY SPIRIT and another SPIRIT that was from Dottie. No message was given; just the fact was known who the anointing was coming from. Sometimes you just know.

JESUS IS NOT BUSY

On the trip to Iowa from Florida and return in 2001, as I have written elsewhere I felt the HOLY SPIRIT'S presence during the entire trip. At one point I said, "How can JESUS take so much time for me?" I heard, *"JESUS is not busy."*

GOD IS DNA

JESUS replied, "Phillip, don't you even yet know WHO I am, even after all the time I have been with you? Anyone who has seen ME has seen the FATHER: So why are you asking to see HIM? Don't you believe that I am in the FATHER and the FATHER is in ME? The words I say are not MY own, but MY FATHER WHO lives in ME, does HIS work through ME. Just believe that I am in the FATHER and the FATHER is in ME. Or at least believe because of what you have seen ME do. (John 14:9-11 NLT)

And as they did eat, JESUS took bread, and blessed, and brake it, and gave to them, and said, Take, eat: This is MY body. And HE took the cup, and when HE had given thanks, HE gave it to them: and they all drank of it. And HE said unto them This is MY blood of the New Testament, which is shed for many. (Mark 14:22-24 KJV)

These two passages support the fact that GOD is DNA.

Now after that John was put in prison, JESUS came into Galilee, preaching the gospel of the Kingdom of GOD; And saying, The time is fulfilled, and the Kingdom of GOD is at hand: Repent ye, and believe the gospel. (Mark 1:14-15 KJV)

This passage indicates that JESUS has entered Heaven on Earth.

The message, *"GOD is DNA,"* occurred in the early 1990s. I had been reading but finished the book and was just sitting looking out the window, when I heard the words. The voice was clear and distinct, but the words made no sense to me. I knew what DNA was at the time.

After the discussion lately about Intelligent Design or Evolution I have been reading about both I. D. and evolution.

The scientists are not sure where DNA came from or how. DNA is the same for plant life (trees, grass) fish, birds and humans. RNA is a messenger for the combining of the male & female genes with DNA. GOD/DNA provides nearly all life. RNA only is found in some bacteria and virus.

PAY ATTENTION TO THIS SCRIPTURE II

Included in Luke 19:41-44 are the following words: *and your children within you.* This phrase extends the prophecy forever for the Hebrews. The Holocaust is included within the time frame and is equally effective today.

THIRD SECTION
My Conclusions

The HOLY SPIRIT is the senior member of the TRINITY. The HOLY SPIRIT exists in space, both near and far.

GOD is DNA: DNA is the molecular basis for heredity. DNA combines the male genes with the female genes for the offspring of plants, fishes, birds, humans and nearly all other living things on Earth. GOD as DNA creates order for life. GOD is the third parent, many times referred to as FATHER in the Bible.

Without the HOLY SPIRIT & GOD/DNA all would be chaos.

People are created in the HOLY SPIRIT'S image. GOD is present in humans both in the flesh and the SPIRIT. Humans were set free to make their own choices. GOD will not over ride our desires. We must become as little children; that is, get our egos, greed and all other garbage out of the way to allow GOD to direct our lives.

JESUS was not born of a virgin. HE was, evidently, the first to allow GOD to shine in HIS full nature, after JEHOVAH limited the life span of people to 120 years.

And the LORD, MY SPIRIT shall not always strive with man, for that he also is flesh; yet his days shall be an hundred and twenty years. (Genesis 6:3 KJV)

The fact that JESUS was a human, just like the rest of us, makes it more impressive that HE was willing to die for our sins.

JESUS replied: "With all the earnestness I possess I tell you this: Unless you are Born Again, you can never get into the Kingdom of GOD." (John 3:3 TLB)

When we are 'Born Again' is when we allow to GOD to manifest HIMSELF in us.

So JESUS told them, "I'm not teaching MY own ideas, but those of GOD WHO sent ME." (John 7:16 NLT)

"I and MY FATHER are ONE." (John 10:30 NKJV)

We each have the same potential as JESUS.

We each have a direct connection with the HOLY SPIRIT. We do not need a paid priest to tell us how to live. In fact a paid priest or minister will delay the process. Only a sincere desire to make the HOLY SPIRIT first in our lives is needed.

The SPIRIT or a spirit can be passed by prayer, hypnosis, certain mushrooms or high emotional experiences. My experience has been those who receive the SPIRIT by prayer, do not grow beyond their level of morality at the time of the prayer.

From the scientist's view, they refer to the Born Again experience as an epiphany caused by a chemical/electrical reaction in the body and they are correct.

I recommend that we allow JESUS/GOD to direct the Born Again experience as stated by the following verses.

"If you love ME, obey MY commandments. And I will ask the FATHER and HE will give you another COUNSELOR, WHO will never leave you. HE is the HOLY SPIRIT, WHO

leads into all truth. The world at large cannot receive **HIM**, because it isn't looking for **HIM** and doesn't recognize **HIM**. But you do, because **HE** lives with you now and later will be in you." (John 14:15-17 NLT)

Do not be guilty of the following:

Give not that which is Holy unto the dogs, neither cast ye your pearls before swine, lest they trample them under their feet, and turn against and rend you. (Matthew 7:6 KJV)

They will not get past Satan as described in Matthew 4. I will quote only a couple of verses here, but all are relevant.

*Again, the devil taketh **HIM** up into an exceeding high mountain, of the world, and the glory of them; and saith unto **HIM**, All these things will I give **THEE**, if thou wilt fall down and worship me.*

*Then saith **JESUS** unto him Get thee hence, Satan: for it is written Thou shalt worship the **LORD** thy **GOD** and **HIM** only shalt thou serve.* (Matthew 4:8-10 KJV)

From my experience, our President Bush is stalled at this stage!

The Hebrews failed to pass this stage of their spiritual growth too, resulting in the loss of the Promise Land. See Luke 19:41-44, the verses I was to: *"Pay attention to this Scripture."*

The Christians denominations also failed this stage in the 4th Century CE. Emperor Constantine was too much of a temptation. They saw in Constantine the possibility of instant growth. The road to failure, of the CHURCH, started when the CHURCH at Rome declared: "Only Peter and his successors have the keys to the Kingdom." And then they misused the 'keys.' The keys are for each of us and they were not given that we might change the HOLY SPIRIT'S plans for us.

How true JESUS was, at the Last Supper, when HE said; *"This is my body and this is MY blood."* A special prayer is not needed to make the bread and wine Holy, they are in fact GOD. Just remember what GOD has provided us with: *All Things.* We need to tend the Garden. Genesis 2:15.

Temple, congregational worship was cancelled by JESUS when HE condemned the Jews and cleansed the Temple in Luke 19:41-48.

"Now, can a divine spirit receive money and still prophesy? It is impossible for a prophet of GOD to do this, but the spirit of such prophets who do so is earthly." (Hermas 43:12)

A person paid to preach is likely to tell people what they want to hear rather than what they need to hear. They cannot afford to loose a single nose because the nickels would stop coming in.

Home worship with the parents teaching is the only solution I see. A few families could join together, but keep the group small enough that *all* participate in the discussion. Each meeting should have a different leader; this will give each person a responsibility. Rotate the meeting leaders among all!!! Our CREATOR set aside the 7th day for rest and to worship HIM. The Sabbath starts at sunset Friday and ends at sunset Saturday.

Music is not necessary. Music can provide a false sense of security.

Ritual carries no influence with GOD, only obedience. We bless ourselves through obedience. "Just A Closer Walk With Thee" is a typical song which gives a false sense of security. HE will bless us as we obey HIM.

GOSPEL OF THOMAS ON THE SABBATH
JESUS said, A person was receiving guests. When he had pre-

pared the dinner, he sent his slave to invite the guests. The slave went to the first and said to that one. "My master invites you."

That one said, "Some merchants owe me money; they are coming tonight. I have to go and give them instructions. Please excuse me from dinner."

The slave went to another and said to that one, "My master invites you."

That one said to the slave, "I have bought a house, and I have been called away for the day. I shall have no time."

The slave went to another and said to that one, "My master invites you."

That one said to the slave, "My friend is to be married, and I am to arrange the banquet. I shall not be able to come. Please excuse me from the dinner."

The slave went to another and said to that one, "My master invites you."

That one said to the slave, "I have bought an estate, and I am going to collect the rent. I shall not be able to come. Please excuse me from the dinner."

The slave returned and said to his master, "Those whom you invited to dinner have asked to be excused."

The master said to his slave, "Go out on the streets and bring back whoever you find to have dinner."

"Buyers and merchants (will) not enter the places of MY FATHER." (64)

I find no restriction on doing chores about the home, on the Sabbath. I travel, in my car, on the Sabbath restricting it to the gas in the car. I do not buy gas for the car on the Sabbath. Eating at the motels that serve a Continental breakfast has met with no objection. Eating out on the Sabbath has been negative.

There are many relief agencies that serve the needy you can give your tithe too. As JESUS said; *"When you do it to least of these you do it to ME."* He was referring to the poor, the hungry, those in prison, the sick, and those in need.

JESUS replied, "And why do you, by your traditions, violate the direct commandments of GOD? For instance, GOD says, 'Honor your father and mother,' And anyone who speaks evil of father or mother must be put to death.' But you say, 'You don't need to honor your parents by caring for their needs if you give the money to GOD instead.' And so, by your own tradition, you nullify the direct commandment of GOD. You hypocrites! Isaiah was prophesying about you when he said, 'These people honor ME with their lips, but their hearts are far away. Their worship is a farce, for they replace GOD'S commands with their own man made teachings.'" (Matthew 15:3-9 NLT)

`Yes, do remember your other family members too.

The government should not have its nose in private matters. The CHURCH should not pry into the individual's affairs since JESUS instructed HIS disciples to shake the dust from their feet if a person did not want to listen to them. (Matthew 10:14)

Abortions: The problem with abortions will end, once adultery and fornication end. Today, there are some abortions that should be and some should not be and a great many that man or woman are not able to judge. There is a male (I am reluctant to use 'man') that is equally guilty if the woman is guilty. GOD can make the proper decision when and if a judgment is to be made.

If a person wants GOD'S help in their marriage they must abstain from pre-martial sex, fornication and adultery. This is the HOLY SPIRIT'S plan for humans, who are created in HIS image. We set out own standards for HIS blessings. Also, remember that our sins are passed to our descendents and associates.

PERFECT

But you are to be perfect, even as your FATHER in Heaven is perfect. (Matthew 5:48 NLT)

Obey GOD because you are HIS children. Don't slip back into your old ways of doing evil; you didn't know any better then. But now you must be Holy in everything you do, just as GOD –WHO chose you to be HIS children—is Holy. For HE HIMSELF has said, "You must be Holy because I am Holy." (1Peter 1:14-16 NLT)

"Not all people who sound religious are really GODLY. The may refer to ME as 'LORD,' but still won't enter the Kingdom of Heaven. The decisive issue is whether they obey MY FATHER in Heaven. On Judgment Day many will tell ME, 'LORD, LORD, we prophesied in YOUR NAME and cast out demons in YOUR NAME.' But I will reply, 'I never knew you. Go away; the things you did were unauthorized.'" (Matthew 7:21-24 NLT)

So the creation of the heavens and the Earth and everything in them was completed. Then the LORD GOD planted a Garden in the east, and there HE placed the man HE had created. The LORD GOD placed the man in the Garden of Eden to tend and care for it. (Genesis 2:1,8,15 NLT)

And to Adam HE said, "Because you listened to your wife and ate the fruit I told you not to eat, I have place a curse on the ground. All you life you will struggle to scratch a living from it." (Genesis 3:17 NLT)

"If you love ME, obey MY commandments. And I will ask the FATHER and HE will give you another COUNSELOR, WHO will never leave you." (John 14:15-16 NLT)

Those who obey MY commandments are the ones who love ME. And because they love ME, MY FATHER will love them, and I will love them, And I will reveal MYSELF to each one of them. (John 14:21 NLT)

`JESUS replied, "All those who love ME will do what I say. MY FATHER will love them, and WE will come to them and live with them. Anyone who doesn't love ME will not do what I say. And remember, MY words are not MY own. This message is from the FATHER WHO sent ME." (John 14:23-24 NLT)

"I tell you this: Whatever you prohibit on Earth is prohibited in Heaven, and whatever you allow on Earth is allowed in Heaven." (Matthew 18:18 NLT)

"He will give you all you need from day to day if you make the Kingdom of GOD your primary concern." (Luke 12:31 NLT)

The steps listed above will lead to Heaven on Earth, if you have **Faith.**

There is only one GOD, and there is only one way of being accepted by HIM. HE makes people right with HIMSELF only by Faith, whether they are Jews or Gentiles. Well then, if we emphasize Faith, does this mean that we can forget about the law? Of course not! Only when we have Faith do we truly fulfill the law. (Romans 3:30-31 NLT)

After we have accepted JESUS and HIS sacrifice the HOLY SPIRIT will remind us of previous sins for which we will be held accountable for. We may need to apologize, make restitution or serve prison time for previous sins. (Bob)

If we try to ignore our problems, by sweeping them under the rug, (hiding them) we will not succeed. GOD lives in us. HIS SPIRIT connects us with all!

DENOMINATIONALISM

"Don't misunderstand why I have come. I did not come to abol-
ish the law or Moses or the writings of the prophets. No, I came
to fulfill them I assure you, until Heaven and Earth disappear,
even the smallest detail of GOD'S law will remain until its
purpose is achieved. So if you break the smallest command-
ment and teach others to do the same, you will be least in the
Kingdom of Heaven.

But I warn you—unless you obey GOD better than the
teachers of religious law and the Pharisees do, you can't enter
the Kingdom of Heaven at all." (Matthew 5:17-20 NLT)

We could substitute any of the denomination's names for
'teachers of religious law and the Pharisees.' Christianity failed
to progress when Matthew 16:19 & 18:18 were misinterpreted
and ignored.

Clinton should have been thrown out of office. Since the
Senate made a moral issue a political issue we got an even worse
man for president. The Senate loosed GOD'S protection.

"War is killing." The average American citizen will suffer
for the Iraq war unless the citizens impeach the leaders and turn
them over to a world court for judgment. Or some such equal
action; we cannot allow the leaders to go unpunished. If the
citizens don't act GOD will remove HIS protection. The history, of the United States' actions in the past, is not blameless.

Jerusalem fell to the Roman Army in 70 AD when the
Zealots had been the leaders for 3½ years.

PSALM 46

GOD is our refuge and strength, always ready to help in times
of trouble.

So we will not fear, even if earthquakes come and the moun-
tains crumble into the sea.

Let the oceans roar and foam. Let the mountains tremble as the waters surge!

A river brings joy to the city of our GOD, the sacred home of the MOST HIGH.

GOD HIMSELF lives in that city; it cannot be destroyed. GOD will protect it at the break of day.

The nations are in an uproar, and kingdoms crumble!

GOD thunders and the Earth melts

The LORD ALMIGHTY is here among us; the GOD of Israel is our fortress.

Come see the glorious works of the LORD: See how HE brings destruction upon the world.

And causes wars to end throughout the Earth. HE breaks the bow and snaps the spear in two; HE burns the shields with fire.

"Be silent, and know that I am GOD! I will be honored by every nation. I will be honored throughout the world."

The LORD ALMIGHTY is here among us; the GOD of Israel is our fortress. (NLT)

Psalm 46 has always been my favorite. It is so appropriate for today. *"GOD HIMSLEF lives in that city."* We are, in fact, that city! *"GOD is DNA!"* *"A river brings joy to the city of our GOD."*

"And causes wars to end." I knew this to be TRUTH, but never expected to be so appropriate in my time.

"The HOLY SPIRIT is the ONE, WHO creates order out of chaos." Bob

Seeing & Entering the Kingdom of Heaven

Not everyone that saith unto ME, LORD, LORD, shall enter into the Kingdom of Heaven; but he that doeth the will of MY FATHER which is in Heaven. Many will say to ME in that day, LORD, LORD, have we not prophesied in THY

NAME? and in THY NAME have cast out devils? and in THY NAME done many wonderful works? and then will I profess unto them, I never knew you; depart from ME, ye that work iniquity. (Matthew 7:21-23 KJV)

A passage from *The Shepherd of Hermas.*

"Tell me, sir," I said, *"the names of the VIRGINS and of the women who dressed in the black garments."*

"Hear," he said, *"the names of the stronger VIRGINS WHO are stationed at the corners. The first is FAITH, and the second, SELF-CONTROL, and the third, POWER, and the fourth, PATIENCE. And the others standing between them have these NAMES: SINCERITY, INNOCENCE, PURITY, CHEERFULNESS, TRUTH, UNDERSTANDING, HARMONY, and LOVE. The one who bears these NAMES and the NAME of the SON OF GOD will be able to enter the Kingdom of GOD.*

"Hear also," he said, *"the names of the women with the black clothes. Of these also four are more powerful. The first is Unbelief, the second, Self-Indulgence, the third, Disobedience, and the fourth, Deceit. And the ones who follow them are called Grief, Evil, Licentiousness, Ill-Temper, Falsehood, Foolishness, Slander, and Hatred.*

"The servant of GOD who bears these names will see the Kingdom of GOD but will not enter it." (Hermas 92:1-3)

This passage from Matthew gives us the same message as the passage from Hermas. I quoted Hermas, to point out that many will see the Kingdom of Heaven but will not enter.

They have stumbled at Matthew 4:1-11:

Then was JESUS led up of the SPIRIT into the wilderness to be tempted of the devil, and when HE had fasted forty days and forty nights, HE was afterward an hungred. And when the tempter came to HIM, he said, If THOU be the SON OF

GOD, command that these stones be made bread.

But HE answered and said, It is written, Man shall not live by bread alone, but by every word that proceedeth out of the mouth of GOD.

Then the devil taketh HIM up into the holy city, and setteth HIM on a pinnacle of the temple, and saith unto HIM, If THOU be the SON OF GOD, cast THYSELF down; for it is written, HE shall give HIS angels charge concerning THEE; and in their hands they shall bear THEE up, lest at any time THOU dash THY foot against a stone.

JESUS said unto him, It is written again, Thou shalt not tempt the LORD thy GOD.

Again, the devil taketh HIM up into an exceeding high mountain, and sheweth HIM all the kingdoms of the world, and the glory of them: and saith unto HIM All these things will I give THEE, if THOU will fall down and worship me.

Then saith JESUS unto him, Get thee hence, Satan; for it is written, Thou shalt worship the LORD thy GOD and HIM only shalt thou serve.

Then the devil leaveth HIM and behold, angels came and ministered unto him. (Matthew 4:1-11 KJV)

People get to this point easily after they have been Born Again or had an epiphany. Satan will give them a blessing; they may be delivered of alcoholism. They may find a new wife. The rewards available are endless. Unfortunately, it is not a blessing it is a trap! They go blissfully on there way assuming every thing is right between them and JESUS.

Satan is just waiting for a more appropriate time. Satan is not particular when we go his way, you can count on Satan to be persistent. Temptation is just around the corner in many disguises.

A FEW FAVORITES

If you love something, set it free.

If it comes back to you it is yours.

This was on a calendar, I had it framed. Today it reminds me this is what the HOLY SPIRIT has done with HIS creation of mankind. We are free to choose. Hopefully many of us will return to HIM.

Vice is monster of so frightful mien,

As to hated needs but to be seen,

Yet familiar with her face,

We first endure, then pity, and then embrace. (Alexander Pope)

This is where humanity is with the marriage, divorce problem today. We are so accustomed to many marriages that we take it for granted that our CREATOR approves. HE does not approve!

What a tangled we weave

When first we practice to deceive. (Author unknown)

The CHURCH leaders have deceived us since the 4th century CE. If I did not have full confidence that the HOLY SPIRIT will help untangle the mess I could not have written this book.

RESIST NOT EVIL

"But I say unto you, That ye resist not evil: but whosoever shall smite thee on thy right cheek, turn to him the other also." Matthew 5:39 KJV

The sooner America turns the other cheek, which is; get all the troops out of Iraq, the better off we will all be. We never should have gone there in the first place.

It is time for someone to demonstrate that Matthew 5:39, words spoken by JESUS are truth! The world has decided that it is better to resist violence than to submit to our CREATOR. The world believes in 'just wars.' We have had 2,000 years of 'just wars,' it is time to try JESUS' plan.

As America announces it plan to withdraw its troops; it should mention the following from the Koran.

"He who doth that which is right, doth it to his own behoof, and whoso doth evil, doth it to his own hurt. Hereafter, to your LORD shall ye be brought back."
Koran Sura 45:14 Translated by J. M. Rodwell

"Verily I say unto you, Whatsoever ye shall bind on Earth shall be bound in Heaven: and whatsoever ye shall loose on Earth shall be loosed in Heaven." Matthew 18:18 KJV

"And I will give unto thee the keys of the Kingdom of Heaven: and whatsoever thou shalt bind on Earth shall be bound in Heaven: and whatsoever thou shalt loose on Earth shall be loosed in Heaven." Matthew 16:19 KJV

The meaning is the same in all three verses. Some other Bible quotes which are basically the same.

"For if ye forgive men their trespasses, your Heavenly FATHER will also forgive you: But if ye forgive not men their trespasses, neither will your FATHER forgive your trespasses." Matthew 6:14-15 KJV

"For with what judgment ye judge, ye shall be judged: and with what measure ye mete, it shall be measured to you again." Matthew 7:2 KJV

"And as ye would that men should do to you, do ye also to them likewise." Luke 6:31 KJV

"Therefore say I unto you, The kingdom of GOD shall be taken from you, and given to a nation bringing forth the fruits thereof." Matthew 21:43 KJV

"For what shall it profit a man, if he shall gain the whole world, and lose his own soul?" Mark 8:36 KJV

Both Christianity and Islam listened to the truth in their early stages and had the Keys to Heaven. Both failed to pass the wilderness test of Matthew 4:1-10. They are both listening to Satan, including the President of the United States.

War is killing, war is evil. The future generations will suffer for the sins of the present generation both in the Christian community and the Muslim community. We must seek common ground between the religions. Otherwise we both will end up with a similar proclamation the Jews received from JESUS in Luke 19:41-46.

And when HE was come near, HE beheld the city (Jerusalem), and wept over it, Saying, If thou hadst known, even thou, at least in this thy day, the things which belong unto thy peace! But now they are hid from thine eyes.

For the days shall come upon thee, that thine enemies shall cast a trench about thee, and compass thee round, and keep thee in on every side, and shall lay thee even with the ground, and thy children within thee; and they shall not leave in thee one stone upon another; because thou knewest not the time of thy visitation. And HE went into the temple, and began to cast out them that sold therein, and them that bought; Saying unto them, It is written, MY House is the house of prayer; but ye have made it a den of thieves. Luke 19:41-46 KJV

"Mankind controls his own future." Bob

"GOD lives in each person both physically and spiritually." Bob

"Heaven is for this lifetime on Earth." Bob

"Yes, JESUS weeps." Bob